HISTORICAL AGES

THE BRONZE AGE

BY EMMA KAISER

Core Library

Cover image: The Bronze Age city of Babylon was said to have many palaces, temples, and massive walls.

An Imprint of Abdo Publishing
abdobooks.com

abdobooks.com

Published by Abdo Publishing, a division of ABDO, PO Box 398166, Minneapolis, Minnesota 55439.

Printed in the United States of America, North Mankato, Minnesota.
102024
012025

Cover Photo: mikroman6/Moment/Getty Images
Interior Photos: Chris Radburn/PA Images/Alamy, 4–5, 43; Chris Radburn/EMPPL PA Wire/AP Images, 7, 9; Science History Images/Alamy, 11; Album/Alamy, 14–15; Ashmolean Museum/Heritage Images/Hulton Archive/Getty Images, 17; Georgios Tsichlis/Shutterstock Images, 18, 45; Heracles Kritikos/Shutterstock Images, 20; Red Line Editorial, 22, 38; mikroman6/Moment/Getty Images, 24–25; Shutterstock Images, 27, 32–33; Khim Hoe Ng/Alamy, 29; Qayssar Hussein/Shutterstock Images, 37

Editor: Laura Stickney
Series Designer: Ryan Gale

Library of Congress Control Number: 2024938378

Publisher's Cataloging-in-Publication Data

Names: Kaiser, Emma, author.
Title: The Bronze Age / by Emma Kaiser
Description: Minneapolis, Minnesota: ABDO Publishing, 2025 | Series: Historical ages | Includes online resources and index.
Identifiers: ISBN 9781098295622 (lib. bdg.) | ISBN 9798384916628 (ebook)
Subjects: LCSH: History, Ancient--Juvenile literature. | Bronze age--Juvenile literature. | Subsistence farming--Juvenile literature. | Land settlement--Juvenile literature. | Weapons, Ancient--Juvenile literature. | Civilization and science--Juvenile literature. | History--Juvenile literature. | Historical archaeology--Juvenile literature. | Anthropology, Prehistoric--Juvenile literature.
Classification: DDC 930.15--dc23

CONTENTS

CHAPTER ONE

A BRONZE AGE DISCOVERY

In the mid-1800s and late 1800s, people began digging at Must Farm. This place is located outside of Peterborough, United Kingdom. The wetland site was used as a quarry. People extracted clay from the ground to make bricks.

Later, in 1999, people investigated the Must Farm site. An archaeologist discovered very old posts sticking out of the ground. When scientists tested the posts, they found that the posts were nearly 3,000 years old.

Selina Davenport, *pictured*, worked with the Cambridge Archaeological Unit to excavate ancient homes at Must Farm in 2015 and 2016.

In 2015 and 2016, a large-scale excavation took place at Must Farm.

Most excavations of this kind reveal only bits and pieces of historical items. But this time, archaeologists discovered the contents of entire homes. They recovered items such as textiles and glass beads that formed a necklace. They also found small cups, bowls, and jars. Some of the pottery even had food still preserved inside. Archaeologists were also able to study the wooden posts that formed the houses, along with the knives and cutting tools used to shape them.

A LOOK INTO THE PAST

The artifacts painted a picture of what likely happened to the Must Farm settlement. Around 850 BCE, a family sat down to dinner. They ate from bowls in their circular wooden house. Their house stood on stilts above a river. Similar houses stood nearby. Suddenly, the family heard a commotion. The house began to smoke, and flames started to creep up the walls around them. The family

The homes discovered at Must Farm are called roundhouses. By studying charred timbers at the site, archaeologists were able to reconstruct what these Bronze Age homes looked like.

dropped everything to escape. They left behind their jewelry, their pottery, and all their other physical possessions. Their dinner sat uneaten in their bowls. The family escaped, but their home collapsed into the river below. The river eventually dried up and no longer exists today. But the objects became preserved in the clay of the riverbed, untouched and unnoticed for centuries.

DISCOVERING TEXTILES

It is very rare to discover any kind of textile, such as clothing, from the Bronze Age. This is because fabric breaks down easily and is usually not preserved for thousands of years. Some ancient textiles were made from wool. At Must Farm, archaeologists discovered textiles made from plants. When the textiles caught on fire, they burned. But they stopped burning as soon as they fell into the river. This combination of burning and moisture preserved the textiles.

The discovery of this settlement revealed important information about a significant time in human history. The Must Farm excavation gave archaeologists a fuller picture of how people lived at that time. The objects helped researchers learn more about the clothes people wore, the tools they used, and the food they ate. The discovery provided a snapshot of everyday life thousands of years ago. The homes and objects preserved in the riverbed came from a historical period called the Bronze Age.

Thousands of well-preserved Bronze Age artifacts were uncovered from the Must Farm site, including more than 100 pottery vessels such as bowls and cups.

THE BRONZE AGE BEGINS

Not everyone agrees about when the Bronze Age took place. Some historians believe it started before 3000 BCE, in about 3300 BCE, and some believe it ended in about 1150 BCE. The Bronze Age came after the Stone Age (2.6 million years ago–3300 BCE). During this period, people used stone or flint to make weapons and tools. But metals gradually replaced stone.

The Bronze Age refers to a time when cultures were using bronze. Bronze is an alloy of tin and copper. This means that when the two metals are mixed together, an entirely new metal is created. Ancient people made

INVENTING THE WHEEL

The first wheel was invented in 3500 BCE. It came from Lower Mesopotamia, which is in what is now modern-day Iraq. The Sumerian people lived in the area. They used solid discs of wood and placed them on axles. These axles rotated, causing the wooden disc to rotate too. Historians believe the Sumerian people used these wheels to make pottery. Eventually, people figured out how to use wheels on carts, wheelbarrows, and chariots. This led to major advancements in transportation and farming.

bronze by heating tin and copper. Then they hammered the metals or melted them together. The resulting bronze was much stronger than tin or copper alone.

Bronze led to many human advancements. The metal's strength meant people could shape it into fierce weapons. An army that used bronze spears or arrowheads had an advantage over an army that used wooden or stone weapons. People could also make more effective tools with bronze. Farmers who used bronze plows were able to plant and harvest

During the Bronze Age, people melted tin and copper to make bronze. They used a process called smelting, which involves heating a material such as rock to extract metal from it.

more crops. This is because bronze was stronger and cut through the soil more easily. During the Bronze Age, many important inventions, such as the wheel, changed the course of human history.

Diverse cultures thrived during the Bronze Age. Important empires formed. Ancient civilizations built structures such as the pyramids in Egypt. Other advancements were made in technology, religion, art, architecture, language, war, and trade. The Bronze Age is also when the first evidence of written language appeared.

Different areas of the world entered the Bronze Age at different times. This is because cultures in Mesopotamia and Greece began using bronze closer to 3000 BCE, while cultures in Northern Europe didn't start using it until about 1900 BCE. As people in certain areas of the world started making bronze, they were able to trade it with other groups. In this way, bronze began to spread to many different areas of the Old World. The Old World refers to Europe, Africa, and Asia. The Bronze Age can be broken down into three different time periods. These are the Early Bronze Age, the Middle Bronze Age, and the Late Bronze Age.

STRAIGHT TO THE SOURCE

Duncan Wilson is chief executive of Historic England. This organization helps fund Bronze Age excavations in England. Wilson discussed the Peterborough discovery site:

> *A dramatic fire 3,000 years ago [preserved underwater] has left to us a frozen moment in time, which gives us a graphic picture of life in the Bronze Age. We are learning more about the food our ancestors ate, and the pottery they used to cook and serve it. We can also get an idea of how different rooms were used. This site is of international significance and its excavation really will transform our understanding of the period.*

Source: "Bronze Age Homes Unearthed in East Anglia." *Historic England*, 12 Jan. 2016, historicengland.org. Accessed 20 Feb. 2024.

BACK IT UP

The author of this passage is using evidence to support a point. Write a paragraph describing the point the author is making. Then write down two or three pieces of evidence the author uses to make the point.

CHAPTER TWO

EARLY BRONZE AGE

The Early Bronze Age was the very beginning of the period. It lasted from roughly 3300 BCE through 2000 BCE. Not everyone agrees with this timeline. Some place the dates earlier or later. During the Early Bronze Age, many important developments in human culture took place. People developed new technology and formed important cities.

One of the first areas to enter the Bronze Age was Mesopotamia. This ancient region

Foundation figures are one Bronze Age artifact discovered in Mesopotamia. These decorative nails or pegs marked the foundations of temples.

made up much of modern-day Iraq and part of Syria. Mesopotamia was the site of many significant Bronze Age cities and civilizations. The Sumerians were one important Mesopotamian group. In around 3100 BCE, the Sumerian people invented a form of writing. It was known as the cuneiform writing system.

The cuneiform writing system used wedge-shaped symbols etched onto tablets. Other cultures in Mesopotamia adopted the system. This was the first known time in history that humans used writing to keep records and tell stories. People used the cuneiform

INVENTING THE PLOW

Some archaeologists believe Sumerians invented the first plow in as early as 3100 BCE. The plow was a soil-cutting tool that could be pulled behind animals such as cattle. The plow revolutionized how people farmed. With plows, farming could be done faster and more efficiently. This meant more food could be grown to feed people. Other cultures began using the Sumerians' plow, and the tool eventually spread around the ancient world.

Sumerians used a tool called a stylus to write cuneiform. Styluses were often made from reeds. To write cuneiform, a person pressed the end of the stylus into the surface of a moist clay tablet.

system for more than 3,000 years. Archaeologists have excavated many stone tablets that contain cuneiform writing from ancient Mesopotamian cultures. Tablets have been found at a site in Bassetki, a city in Iraq. Archaeologists have also discovered bronze and metal artifacts, such as vessels, armor, and weapons, at other Early Bronze Age Mesopotamian sites.

Today, people can visit the ruins of the Minoan palace of Knossos in Crete. The site includes reconstructed portions of the palace, such as the West Bastion, *pictured*.

THE MINOAN PEOPLE

Another center of civilization during the Early Bronze Age was the island of Crete. The Minoan people lived on the island. This island is located in the Mediterranean Sea and is now part of modern-day Greece. The Minoans were seafarers. This meant they relied on the sea for their way of life. Minoans traveled across the Mediterranean Sea to trade goods with other nearby cultures, such as the Egyptians.

The Minoans were known for building large, elaborate palaces. These structures were made of interconnected buildings that housed thousands of people. The structures were highly decorated and painted with artwork. The paintings on the palace walls are called frescoes. These frescoes featured many images, including athletes, animals, mythical creatures, and goddesses. Minoan Bronze Age art has also been found outside of Crete in places such as Egypt. This suggests that Minoan art was valuable to other cultures and possibly an item of trade. The Minoans also used bronze for artistic purposes, such as making figurines and decorative vessels. They used the metal to make weapons and tools too.

One of the most famous Minoan palaces is the palace of Knossos. It was believed to be the capital of Crete. The palace was extremely large and complex. It had multiple stories and contained a throne room, a central courtyard, and a theater. It was full of art and colorful, decorative walls. In 1900 CE, British

The colorful frescoes of Knossos help archaeologists learn about Minoan life during the Bronze Age. Many Minoan frescoes feature animals such as dolphins.

archaeologist Arthur Evans began excavating the site of Knossos near Crete's northern coast. Today, people can visit the palace ruins. Studying the ruins has helped archaeologists learn about what the palace once looked like and how people lived during the height of the Minoan civilization.

THE INDUS RIVER VALLEY

The Indus River valley extends across parts of modern-day Afghanistan, Pakistan, and India. It was home to the farthest-extending civilization of the Early

Bronze Age. The Indus River valley civilization began in around 3300 BCE and may have included as many as five million people. The Indus River valley people were known for their urban planning. This refers to the process of planning out and structuring cities. As of 2024, more than 1,052 Bronze Age cities and settlements have been discovered in the Indus River valley.

These cities were made up of baked-brick houses and used advanced water supply and drainage systems. People in the cities built public baths, sewage systems, and walls.

MYTH OF THE MINOTAUR

According to Greek mythology, the palace of Knossos was built at the request of King Minos. He wanted the design of the palace to be so complex that no one could find the exit. Many people associate Knossos with the myth of the minotaur and the labyrinth. A minotaur is a creature with the body of a man and the head of a bull. The minotaur was believed to roam the mazelike palace. King Minos sacrificed people to the monster until it was killed by a hero named Theseus.

EARLY BRONZE AGE EMPIRES

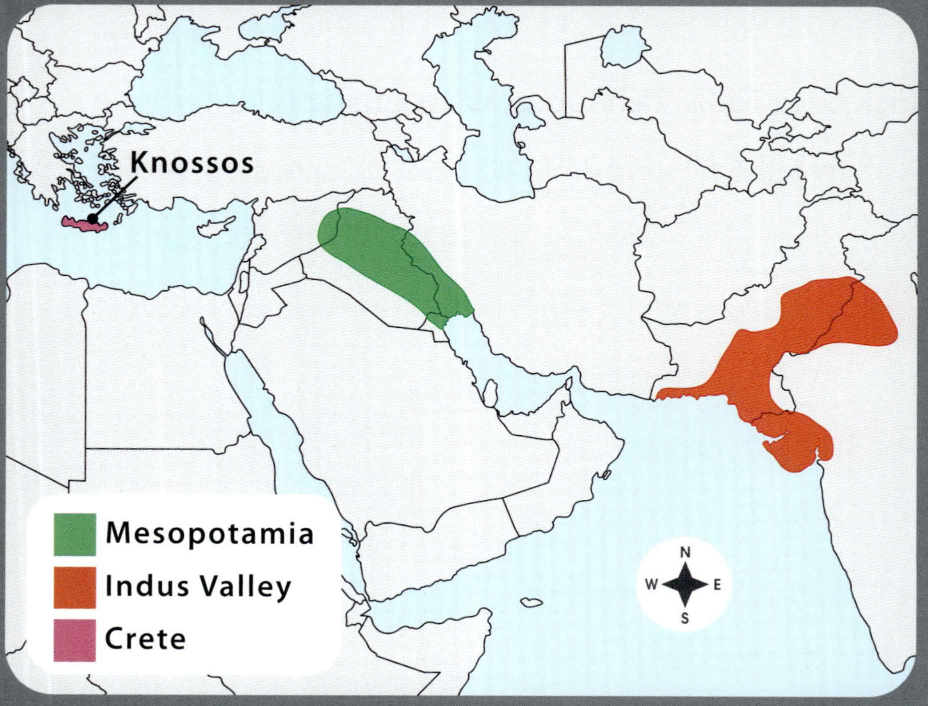

This map shows the major Early Bronze Age civilizations that existed from 3000 to 2000 BCE. What do you notice about where these civilizations were located? Why do you think people settled in these locations?

The Indus River valley people were some of the first to develop sanitation systems for their cities. These systems were more efficient and advanced than those of other cultures at the time. Homes drew water from wells, and wastewater was drained through a system of underground pipes and chutes. Indus River valley people also used bronze to make many different things, including tools, fishhooks, weapons, and jewelry.

In 1856 CE, workers building a railway in India discovered hundreds of thousands of baked bricks. The bricks were uniform and appeared to be very old. The workers didn't realize that they had discovered ruins from the Indus River valley civilization. Later, in the 1920s, archaeologists excavated the site. They found artwork, stone vessels, and the ruins of entire cities. Large public baths and water reservoirs, or human-made lakes, were also discovered.

EXPLORE ONLINE

Chapter Two discusses the civilizations of the Early Bronze Age. The website below explores how the use of bronze led to the first early civilizations. As you know, every source is different. How is the information from the website similar to the information in Chapter Two? What new information did you learn from the website?

BRONZE AGE

abdocorelibrary.com/bronze-age

CHAPTER THREE

MIDDLE BRONZE AGE

The Middle Bronze Age lasted from roughly 2000 BCE through 1600 BCE. More cultures of the ancient world began creating, using, and trading bronze. Human technology and civilizations continued to develop and interact.

While the Minoans were thriving on Crete, another culture developed nearby in mainland Greece. This area was home to the Mycenaean people, who lived during the late Middle Bronze Age and Late Bronze Age.

The city of Mycenae is protected by stone walls. People call the entrance Lion Gate because there are two lions carved into the stone above the opening.

TROJAN WAR

The myth of the Trojan War is based on the Mycenaeans. Legend says that the prince of Troy kidnapped a woman named Helen, who was married to the Greek prince of Sparta. The Greeks sailed across the sea to wage war against the city of Troy, which was in what is now modern-day Turkey. The Greeks tricked the Trojans. They pretended to give them a giant wooden horse as a gift. Members of the Greek army hid inside the horse. The Trojans took it inside the city gates, thinking they had won. But when night fell, the soldiers inside the horse opened the city gates for the rest of the army. The Greeks defeated the Trojans.

Like the Minoans, the Mycenaeans were seafaring people. They relied on ships for trading. Unlike the Minoans, the Mycenaeans were raiders who used their ships to attack or wage war against neighboring groups. Because Greece was rocky and mountainous, farming was difficult. Many Mycenaeans turned to raiding to gain money and goods.

Mycenaean wars and heroes were often celebrated in

Archaeologists have discovered many artifacts in Mycenae, including bronze swords and daggers. Some of these artifacts are displayed at the National Archaeological Museum in Athens, Greece.

ancient texts and myths. Some of the most prominent Mycenaean cities included Thebes, Sparta, Athens, and Mycenae. Mycenaean pottery has been found in Egypt and Mesopotamia, which shows how far trade extended at the time.

EUROPE ENTERS THE BRONZE AGE

In about 2500 BCE, areas of Europe began entering the Bronze Age. In Scotland, several archaeological discoveries have revealed how people lived during the period and how they were treated after death. In the 1890s, people discovered a Middle Bronze

UNEARTHING AVA

In 1987, a Bronze Age burial site was unearthed in Scotland. In 2014, archaeologist Maya Hoole used technology to learn more about the human remains found at the site. Hoole discovered that the body was a young woman who likely died between 2300 BCE and 2145 BCE. Researchers called the Bronze Age woman "Ava." She was between 18 and 25 years old when she died, and DNA testing found that she had dark brown hair and brown eyes. Testing also revealed that Ava ate lots of meat and was lactose intolerant. Archaeologists are unsure of how Ava died. But she was found buried with pollen from plants that were used to treat wounds.

Age settlement in Jarlshof, Scotland. The site features the ruins of many homes from at least 2000 BCE. The homes were oval shaped and made of stone. Most homes had multiple rooms that served different purposes. One stone house had been turned into a workshop for a bronzesmith at the end of the Bronze Age. He made swords, axes, and other tools there.

In 2009, archaeologists found a gravesite located

At Flag Fen Archaeological Park in Peterborough, England, visitors can go inside a reconstructed Bronze Age roundhouse.

near Perthshire, Scotland. It was clear that the gravesite belonged to an important Bronze Age individual. The body had been laid on a bed of quartz pebbles inside a large stone coffin. The person was buried alongside a bronze dagger that was kept in a sheath.

The grave was so well preserved that plant material was still present in the coffin. Archaeologists found evidence that people had laid flowers on the person's grave. The person had also been buried among other important Scottish Bronze Age monuments, which suggested that the person was highly respected by the community.

CHINA'S MYTHICAL PERIOD

By around 2000 BCE, a unified Chinese culture began developing in areas along the Yellow River. Much of what archaeologists know about China in the Middle Bronze Age comes from ancient Chinese historians. Some modern historians believe this early history is made up of myths. Others believe there is truth behind it. Because of the uncertainty, this period is sometimes referred to as China's mythical period.

The Xia Dynasty is described as the first Chinese dynasty. The Xia Dynasty possibly began in 2070 BCE. Its early rulers are credited with developing silk production, making advancements in medicine and farming, and inventing musical instruments.

Whether the Xia Dynasty existed or not, bronze was an important part of ancient Chinese culture. While other Bronze Age cultures used bronze mainly for weapons and tools, people in China used it mostly for artistic work. Bronze vessels were a symbol of power and wealth, and some were reserved only for rulers. The vessels played an important role in rituals and religious worship. The Chinese had a unique way of working with bronze that differed from other cultures. They melted the metal and poured it into casts, or molds of certain shapes. When the bronze had cooled and hardened, they removed the casts.

FURTHER EVIDENCE

Chapter Three discusses Chinese civilizations that developed during the Middle Bronze Age. Some historians debate whether information about early Chinese dynasties is based on facts or myths. What is the main point of this chapter? What key evidence supports this point? Go to the article about Chinese dynasties at the website below. Find a quote from the website that supports the chapter's main point.

IMPERIAL CHINA'S DYNASTIES

abdocorelibrary.com/bronze-age

CHAPTER FOUR

LATE BRONZE AGE

The final period of the Bronze Age is the Late Bronze Age. It spanned from roughly 1600 BCE to 1200 BCE. By this time, many civilizations had reached their peak. Settlements turned into cities, and some cities turned into empires. Many civilizations had their own writing systems. They traded goods with other empires and made their own forms of art and pottery.

One civilization that reached the height of its power during this period was Egypt.

Karnak in Luxor, Egypt, is part of a large temple complex. It includes the Avenue of Sphinxes, a walkway featuring rows of ancient statues.

THE PYRAMIDS OF GIZA

Egypt's famous pyramids were built during the Bronze Age. Three of the best-known pyramids are the Pyramids of Giza, built roughly 4,500 years ago. Ancient kings were buried inside them. The largest pyramid, known as the Great Pyramid, was 480 feet (146 m) tall and built with 2.3 million blocks of stone. By the time of Egypt's New Kingdom, people started burying pharaohs in tombs rather than in pyramids. Some historians think this was to prevent grave robbers from stealing the treasures the rulers were buried with.

During the Bronze Age, Egypt entered periods known as the Old Kingdom, the Middle Kingdom, and the New Kingdom. The New Kingdom lasted from about 1500 BCE to 1000 BCE.

The New Kingdom is one of the best-known periods of ancient Egyptian history. During this time, Egyptian rulers became known as pharaohs. Notable pharaohs who ruled during Egypt's New Kingdom include Hatshepsut, Tutankhamun, Thutmose III, and Ramses II.

The New Kingdom is one of the most well-documented eras of Egyptian history. This is because more people were reading and writing at the time than ever before. Egyptians were also in contact with other civilizations. Many of their contracts, treaties, sale records, and letters were documented and preserved. Because of Egypt's wealth, power, and trade relationships with other empires, historians consider the kingdom part of the Club of Great Powers. This refers to a group of powerful Bronze Age civilizations.

Egypt controlled some of the largest gold mines in the ancient world. Late Bronze Age Egyptians also used bronze to make statues and figurines, knives, and dishes. Many pharaohs used their wealth to build or contribute to remarkable structures and works of art. Temples were important buildings made to honor gods. One of the most impressive was the temple at Karnak. It was built to honor the chief god, Amon-Re. Many pharaohs added to or expanded the temple. It included dozens of massive stone pillars, a great hall, and walls carved with hieroglyphics. These are symbols that make up an Egyptian writing system. Today, people can visit many temple structures at Karnak.

THE CITY OF BABYLON

The city of Babylon was also part of the Club of Great Powers during the Late Bronze Age. At one point, Babylon was considered the center of Mesopotamian civilization. The city is located near the Euphrates River in modern-day Iraq. One of Babylon's most famous rulers was Hammurabi. He transformed the small city into a great empire. Hammurabi is also famous for creating a system of laws. This created guidelines that judges could follow when deciding on punishments for people who broke laws.

Little is known about what Babylon looked like during Hammurabi's rule. There is little archaeological evidence. However, historians have discovered ancient texts that provide some information about Babylon during the Late Bronze Age. After Hammurabi's

Today, people who visit Babylon can see the ruins of the city alongside reconstructed portions of its walls. The city became a UNESCO World Heritage Site in 2019.

death, armies and empires fought over control of the city. Around 1550 BCE, the Kassite people took over Babylon. For a time, the region experienced peace and prosperity. The Kassites traded with other empires, such as Egypt, and different goods spread across the region. The Kassites ruled for more than 500 years. They introduced horses to Babylon.

EARLY HISTORICAL PERIODS

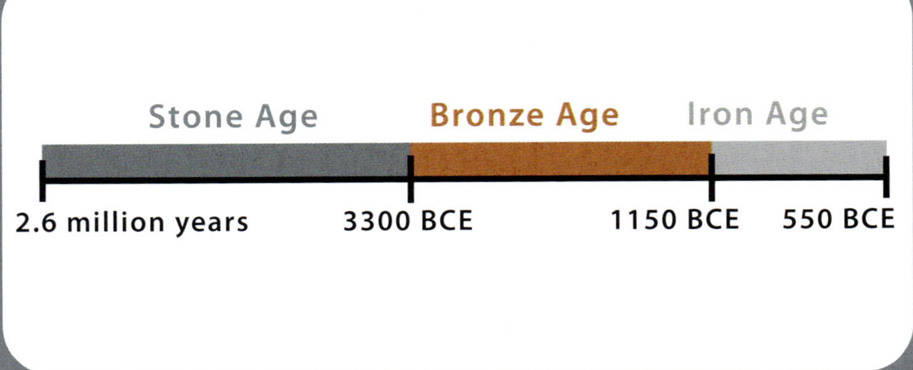

This timeline shows the dates of major historical periods. What do you notice about where the Bronze Age falls on the timeline? Which periods came before and after the Bronze Age?

COLLAPSE OF THE BRONZE AGE

The Bronze Age collapse lasted from roughly 1200 BCE to 1150 BCE. During this time, some of the most powerful Bronze Age civilizations began to break down and decline. Widespread disasters and deaths took place on a large scale. Long-established trade relationships ended, and writing systems disappeared. Archaeologists don't know exactly what caused the collapse of the Bronze Age, but there are a few theories. Most historians believe that several factors led to the collapse.

Archaeological evidence suggests that several natural disasters took place at the time. Archaeologists have determined that warmer temperatures caused droughts. Ancient written records from the Egyptians and the Hittites mention that droughts destroyed crops, which started famines. In letters written by Late Bronze Age rulers, the rulers begged other groups to give them grain to feed their people. Earthquakes may have also hit regions of Greece, which could have produced destructive tidal waves that affected the Minoans and Mycenaeans.

Other evidence suggests that empires were attacked by foreign invaders. It's unclear where these invaders came from, but they are often referred to as the Sea People. While Egypt appeared to defeat the invaders, other invaders weakened the cities of Greece and areas of Mesopotamia. These environmental and political events left many empires unstable.

After the collapse, many regions entered a dark age. Language, art, architecture, and other aspects

DARK AGE

Evidence suggests that toward the end of the Bronze Age, many cities became dirty and unsanitary. People abandoned them and moved to more remote areas. Instead of building homes out of brick or stone, they began building them out of mud. While writing was important for trade and business, the decline of cities and empires meant that many types of writing were lost. Because many people were struggling and starving, they couldn't afford to buy or make art. It would take a long time for people to recover and for new empires to emerge.

of life declined.

Eventually, iron became a more popular metal and gradually replaced bronze. This may have been because iron was more durable and more readily available. This change marked the end of the Bronze Age and the beginning of the Iron Age.

STRAIGHT TO THE SOURCE

Eric H. Cline is a professor of classical and ancient Near Eastern studies at George Washington University. He wrote a book about the Bronze Age collapse. In an interview, he said:

> *There must have been a "perfect storm" of calamitous events at that turning point in order to cause the Late Bronze Age civilizations to collapse shortly after 1200 BCE. There is . . . evidence that there was climate change, drought and famine, earthquakes, invasions and internal rebellions. . . . [Civilizations] were not able to weather the "perfect storm" of nearly simultaneous catastrophes, with each . . . piling on misfortune after misfortune until the entire system broke down. And then what we see is a systems' collapse, as empires and kingdoms that had flourished for centuries all came to an end.*

Source: James Blake Wiener. "Interview: The Mysterious Bronze Age Collapse with Eric Cline." *World History Encyclopedia*, 19 Sep. 2019, worldhistory.org. Accessed 29 Feb. 2024.

WHAT'S THE BIG IDEA?

Take a close look at this passage. What is the main connection being made between disasters and the Bronze Age collapse? How did these disasters cause the decline of Bronze Age civilizations?

IMPORTANT DATES

3500 BCE
People in Mesopotamia invent the wheel.

3300 BCE
The Early Bronze Age begins.

2000 BCE
The Middle Bronze Age begins.

1600 BCE
The Late Bronze Age begins.

1500 BCE
The New Kingdom of Egypt begins.

1200–1150 BCE
Bronze Age civilizations collapse due to several environmental and political factors.

1200–1000 BCE
Iron begins to replace bronze. The Iron Age begins.

850 BCE
The Bronze Age settlement of Must Farm, located in modern-day England, collapses into the river below.

1900 CE
Arthur Evans excavates the site of Knossos in northern Crete.

1999
People investigate the Must Farm site.

2015–2016
A full excavation of the Must Farm site begins.

STOP AND THINK

Dig Deeper

After reading this book, what questions do you still have about how the use of bronze changed the world? With an adult's help, find a few reliable sources that can help you answer your questions. Write a paragraph about what you learned.

Why Do I Care?

The Bronze Age happened thousands of years ago. But that doesn't mean you can't think about why this period was important. What Bronze Age inventions changed life for people? What Bronze Age inventions do you still use today?

You Are There

This book discusses ancient civilizations of the Bronze Age. Imagine you are traveling back in time. Write a letter home telling your friends about the Bronze Age cities you visit. What do you notice about the cities? Be sure to add plenty of detail to your notes.

Take a Stand

Archaeologists often disagree about what ancient texts or archaeological evidence tell us about history. Some think historical accounts from myths are untrustworthy. Others think these accounts should be taken more seriously because they hold elements of historical events. Do you think myths and stories can tell important things about people who lived long ago? Or should researchers rely mostly on physical evidence? Why or why not?

GLOSSARY

archaeologist
a person who studies human history through artifacts and other remains

civilization
a stage of advanced human culture and development

dynasty
a line of rulers who are related to each other

environmental
of or relating to nature

excavation
the act of digging up the ground to uncover artifacts or remains

flint
a type of hard, gray rock

monument
a structure built to remind people of a person or event

political
of or relating to how a country is ruled or governed

quarry
a deep pit where stone or another material is dug up

raider
a person who attacks or steals from others

sanitation
the practice of creating clean living conditions for people

textile
a piece of clothing or fabric

urban
of or relating to cities

ONLINE RESOURCES

To learn more about the Bronze Age, visit our free resource websites below.

Visit **abdocorelibrary.com** or scan this QR code for free Common Core resources for teachers and students, including vetted activities, multimedia, and booklinks, for deeper subject comprehension.

Visit **abdobooklinks.com** or scan this QR code for free additional online weblinks for further learning. These links are routinely monitored and updated to provide the most current information available.

LEARN MORE

Dickmann, Nancy. *Amazing Ancient World Atlas*. Lonely Planet, 2024.

Howell, Izzi. *The Genius of the Stone, Bronze, and Iron Ages*. Crabtree, 2020.

INDEX

About the Author

Emma Kaiser is a writer and educator based in western Minnesota. She has a master of fine arts degree in creative writing from the University of Minnesota, and her writing has appeared in several magazines and other publications. She is the author of several nonfiction books for students.